Safari Animals™

WILDEBEESTS

Katherine Walden

PowerKiDS
press™

New York

Published in 2009 by The Rosen Publishing Group, Inc.
29 East 21st Street, New York, NY 10010

First Edition

Editor: Amelie von Zumbusch
Book Design: Erica Clendening
Layout Design: Julio Gil
Photo Researcher: Jessica Gerweck

Photo Credits: All images Shutterstock.com.

Library of Congress Cataloging-in-Publication Data

Walden, Katherine.
  Wildebeests / Katherine Walden. — 1st ed.
     p. cm. — (Safari animals)
  Includes index.
  ISBN 978-1-4358-2692-2 (library binding) — ISBN 978-1-4358-3066-0 (pbk.)
ISBN 978-1-4358-3078-3 (6-pack)
  1. Gnus—Juvenile literature. I. Title.
  QL737.U53W24 2009
  599.64'59—dc22
                                        2008021587

Manufactured in the United States of America

CPSIA Compliance Information: Batch #W114130PK:
For Further Information contact Rosen Publishing, New York, New York at 1-800-237-9932

CONTENTS

This animal may look like a hairy cow, but it is really a wildebeest! Wildebeests are also known as gnus.

Wildebeests are big animals. They can weigh as much as 600 pounds (272 kg).

Each wildebeest has a pair of **horns**. Wildebeests also have manes and **beards**.

9

Wildebeests live on the grasslands and open woodlands of Africa.

Some animals hunt wildebeests. Wildebeests run as fast as 50 miles per hour (80 km/h) to escape their enemies!

Baby wildebeests are called **calves**. Wildebeest calves can stand just minutes after they are born!

Newborn wildebeests drink their mothers' milk. Older wildebeests eat grass.

When there is plenty of grass to eat, wildebeests live in small groups.

In the dry season, huge wildebeest **herds** form. The animals travel in search of new grass.

The wildebeests cross rivers and travel as far as several thousand miles (km) to find grass to eat.

Words to Know

beard

calf

herd

horn

Index

Web Sites

Due to the changing nature of Internet links, PowerKids Press has developed an online list of Web sites related to the subject of this book. This site is updated regularly. Please use this link to access the list:
www.powerkidslinks.com/safari/wildeb/